by Tanya Thayer

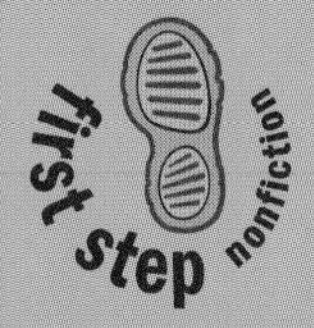

It is winter.

It is cold.

The days are short.

Most trees do not have leaves.

Bears sleep.

People stay warm.

Foxes **hunt** for food.

People eat warm food.

Lakes **freeze.**

Children skate.

Animals have warm coats.

People have warm clothes.

Animals dig for food.

Icicles start to **melt.**

Sap starts to **flow** from trees.

Spring is coming.

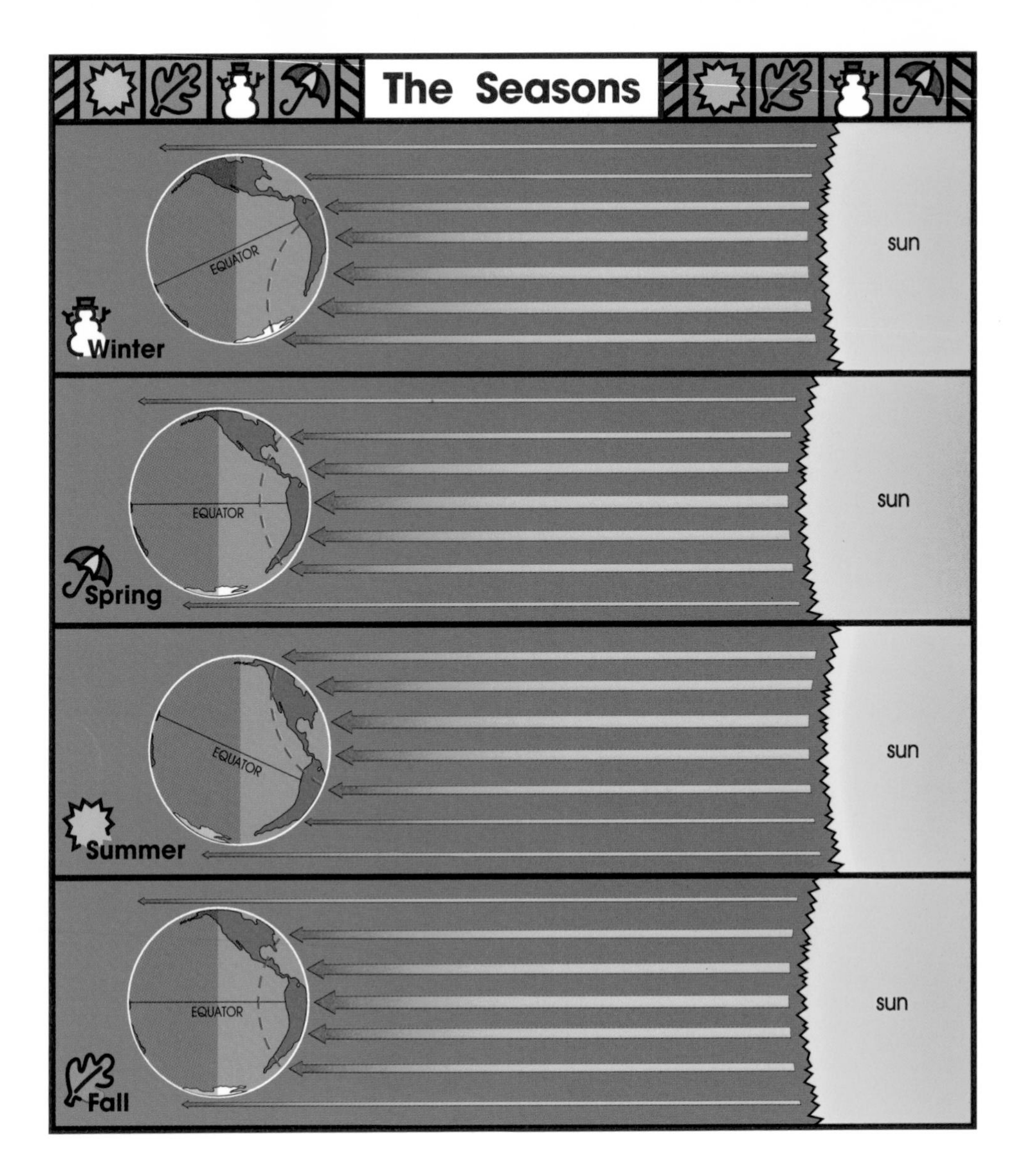
The Seasons
sun
EQUATOR
Winter
sun
EQUATOR
Spring
sun
EQUATOR
Summer
sun
EQUATOR
Fall

Seasons

The earth moves around the sun. The sun shines on the earth. When the sun shines mostly on the southern half of the world, it is winter in the United States.

There is less sunlight in the winter than there is in the fall. The days are shorter in the winter, too. When there is less sunlight in a day, it is colder.

Winter Facts

In some parts of the world, it feels like winter all year.

Some animals grow white fur or feathers in the winter. Animals that are white are harder to see in the snow. They are camouflaged in the snow.

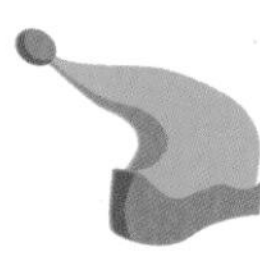

Food is harder for animals to find in the winter. Some animals cannot find enough food to live.

Trees that do not have leaves in the winter are dormant. Dormant means that the tree does not grow. The dormant tree will grow again in the spring.

Some animals stay warm and healthy by sleeping in a den all winter. Animals that sleep all winter are hibernating.

Glossary

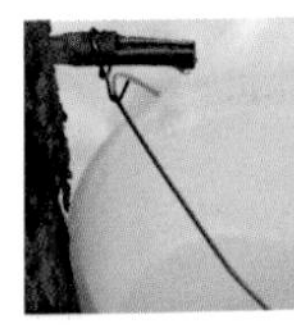

flow - to move in a stream

freeze - when a liquid becomes a solid

hunt - to look for food

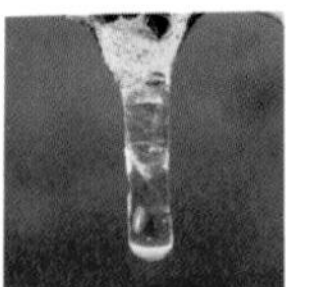

melt - when a solid becomes a liquid

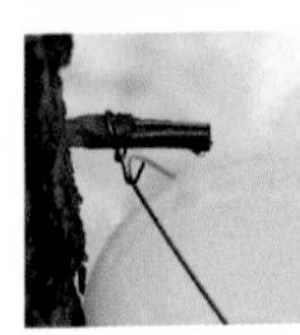

sap - the water inside a plant

Index

The photographs in this book are reproduced through the courtesy of:
©Robert Fried, front cover; ©National Science Foundation, p. 2; ©Clark Mishler/Corbis, p. 3; ©John Kohout/Root Resources, p. 4; ©Stephen Graham Photography p. 5; ©Tom J. Ulrich/Visuals Unlimited, p. 6; ©Danny Lehman/Corbis, p. 7; ©Michele Burgess, pp. 8, 22 (middle); ©Corbis, p. 9; ©Stephen G. Donaldson, pp. 10, 22 (second from top); ©MacDonald Photography/Root Resources, p. 11; ©Paulette Johnson, p. 12; ©Joseph Sohm; ChromoSohm Inc./Corbis, p. 13; ©Ed Kashi, p. 14; ©Richard Cummins, pp. 15, 22 (second from bottom); ©D. Richter MTV/Visuals Unlimited, Inc, pp. 16, 22 (top, bottom); ©D. Yeske/Visuals Unlimited, p. 17.

This book is available in two editions:
Library binding by Lerner Publications Company, a division of Lerner Publishing Group
Soft cover by First Avenue Editions, an imprint of Lerner Publishing Group
241 First Avenue North
Minneapolis, MN 55401 USA

Website address: www.lernerbooks.com

Library of Congress Cataloging-in-Publication Data

Thayer, Tanya.
Winter/ by Tanya Thayer.
p. cm. — (First step nonfiction)
Includes index.
ISBN 0-8225-1985-2 (lib. bdg.: alk. paper)
ISBN 0-8225-1989-5 (pbk.: alk. paper)
1. Winter—Juvenile literature. [1. Winter.] I. Title. II. Series.
QB637.8.T48 2002
508.2—dc21 2001000538

Manufactured in the United States of America
1 2 3 4 5 6 – AM – 07 06 05 04 03 02